FOCUS ON CURRENT EVENTS

MASS INCARCERATION

by Tom Head

FOCUS READERS.

V@YAGER

www.focusreaders.com

Focus Readers is distributed by North Star Editions:
sales@northstareditions.com | 888-417-0195

Produced for Focus Readers by Red Line Editorial.

Content Consultant: Holly Foster, PhD, Professor of Sociology, Texas A&M University

Photographs ©: Shutterstock Images, cover, 1, 7 (left), 7 (right), 8–9, 10, 14–15, 23, 26–27, 40–41, 43, 45; Eric Risberg/AP Images, 4–5; Wally Santana/AP Images, 12; LM Otero/AP Images, 17; Reed Saxon/AP Images, 18–19; Harvey Georges/AP Images, 21; Rob Carr/AP Images, 25; Spencer Weiner/Pool Los Angeles Times/AP Images, 28; Red Line Editorial, 31; Sean Murphy/AP Images, 33; Tony Dejak/AP Images, 34–35; Joshua Polson/The Greeley Tribune/AP Images, 37; Karla Ann Cote/NurPhoto/AP Images, 39

Library of Congress Cataloging-in-Publication Data
Library of Congress Cataloging-in-Publication Data is available on the Library of Congress website.

ISBN
978-1-63739-642-1 (hardcover)
978-1-63739-699-5 (paperback)
978-1-63739-806-7 (ebook pdf)
978-1-63739-756-5 (hosted ebook)

Printed in the United States of America
Mankato, MN
082023

ABOUT THE AUTHOR

Tom Head, PhD, has written or co-written three dozen nonfiction books on a wide range of subjects, including *Crime and Punishment in America* (Facts On File/Infobase), *The Scottsboro Boys* (Abdo), and *Civil Liberties: A Beginner's Guide* (Oneworld). He lives in Jackson, Mississippi, where he works as a chaplain.

TABLE OF CONTENTS

CHAPTER 1

THE LAND OF PRISONS

The United States is home to only 4 percent of the world's population. However, the country holds nearly 16 percent of the world's prisoners. The United States imprisons people at five times the world average. It has done so for decades. As of 2023, there were approximately 1.7 million people behind bars in the United States. That is more than the total populations of 11 states.

The number of people in US prisons is greater than the total population of many countries.

China and the United States have a similar number of prisoners. However, China's overall population is more than four times that of the United States. So, the United States has a much higher rate of **incarceration** than China. Meanwhile, the United States has three times as many prisoners as India. Yet India's population is four times larger.

Some US lawmakers believe too many Americans are sent to prison. They also note **disparities** in prison sentences. On average, Black and Latino people go to prison more often than white people who are **convicted** of the same crimes. In addition, Black and Latino people tend to receive longer sentences. Similarly, low-income people go to prison more often than wealthy people who are convicted of the same crimes. Low-income people also receive longer sentences.

However, other lawmakers think the United States does not imprison enough people. These lawmakers say more people need to be put behind bars. They believe this will make the country safer. For this reason, they push for laws that create longer prison sentences. They also want to increase the number of crimes that require prison sentences.

BY THE NUMBERS ◀

US percent of world's population

4.3%

US percent of world's prisoners

15.7%

Statistics accurate as of 2023.

CHAPTER 2

PUNISHMENT BEFORE PRISONS

The first modern prisons were built in the early 1800s. Before that, incarceration was not a common punishment. People were locked up in jail cells for brief periods. But they stayed there only while they waited for their punishments. The most common punishments included death, fines, slavery, maiming, torture, and exile.

The death penalty was once very common. In the 1800s, people in the United Kingdom

The ancient city of Ur had the world's oldest known set of laws. Most crimes were punished by fines.

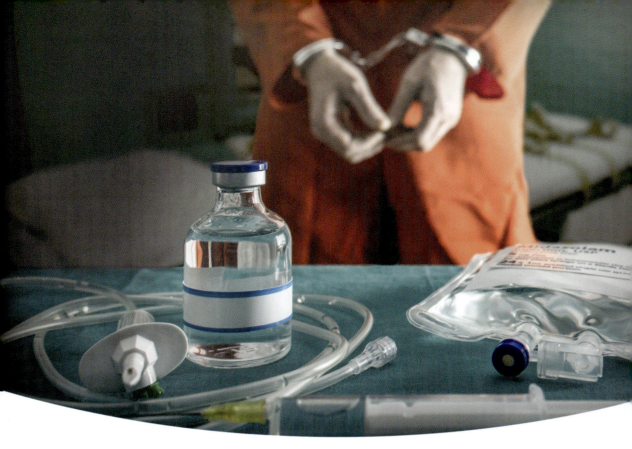

△ Today, lethal injection is the most common way that US states carry out the death penalty.

could be executed for more than 200 crimes. These included stealing a handkerchief, fishing in the wrong lake, or setting fire to hay. Children as young as seven could be executed. Today, the death penalty is illegal in most countries. However, it is still used in many US states.

Fines were used as another common form of punishment. People could be fined either money or property. Those who could not afford to pay their fines were sometimes enslaved.

Slavery is an old punishment. Sometimes the person was enslaved for the rest of his or her life. Sometimes it was for a specific period of time. The Thirteenth Amendment to the Constitution ended slavery in the United States. But the amendment still allows forced labor as punishment for a crime.

Maiming was also a common form of punishment. A person might have an ear, nose, finger, hand, or foot cut off. In the 1600s and 1700s, the removal of ears was used in the American colonies.

Torture was once a common punishment as well. People could be beaten, whipped, cut, or

△ In the early 2000s, US soldiers tortured people at Abu Ghraib prison in Iraq.

burned. They could even be partially drowned or stretched out. Today, torture is illegal in the United States. However, US soldiers and police officers have been caught using torture in modern times.

Exile is one of the oldest punishments. A person was sent away from the community and not allowed to return. In many cases, the person had no way of traveling to another city. As a result, exile could result in death.

During the 1700s and 1800s, many leaders began to see death, slavery, maiming, and torture as cruel. So, they looked for other options. Their ideas about prisons often focused on education and self-reflection. Some of the first prisons were called penitentiaries. Their founders believed spending time alone would make people penitent. That is a feeling of shame and a desire for forgiveness. Over time, imprisonment replaced most other forms of punishment.

THINK ABOUT IT ◁

The Eighth Amendment to the Constitution bans cruel and unusual punishment. Can you think of effective punishments that are not cruel or unusual?

CHAPTER 3

THE PRISON SYSTEM

ost early prisons were based on one of two models. The Pennsylvania model followed the example of Eastern State Penitentiary in Philadelphia. This prison was founded by deeply religious Quakers in 1829. It focused on **solitary confinement**, education, and silence. The Quakers believed prisoners would develop healthier habits if they were kept by themselves. That way, the prisoners could avoid negative influences.

Eastern State Penitentiary closed in 1971. It is now a museum.

In contrast, the New York model followed the example of Auburn Prison. There, prisoners did not sit separately in silence. Instead, they worked together in silence. Prisoners received whippings if they did not follow the rules. This approach offered several advantages to the people who ran the prison. First, it allowed them to fit more prisoners into the same amount of space. Second, hard work kept the prisoners tired. That way, prisoners would be unlikely to fight back. Third, the system was profitable. The prisoners' labor brought in money. Gradually, the New York model began to take over as the most common system in the United States.

Over the next century, prison **reformers** worked to reduce the use of whippings. They also reduced the amount of time people spent in solitary confinement. Meanwhile, the US prison

▲ Today, most experts believe solitary confinement is harmful to people's physical and mental health.

population slowly increased. It topped 100,000 by 1930. And by 1960, there were more than 200,000 prisoners. This number had dropped slightly by 1970. However, the decrease proved to be short-lived. During this period, lawmakers passed tough new state and **federal** laws. As a result, the prison population rose sharply between 1970 and 2000. This began the era of mass incarceration in the United States.

CHAPTER 4

DRUGS AND RACISM

In 1970, the United States housed fewer than 200,000 prisoners. But by 2000, more than 1.9 million Americans were behind bars. In only 30 years, the country's prison population multiplied by nearly 10. Experts still debate the exact reasons for this huge increase. They point to several causes.

One possible reason was the improvement in police tools. These tools included electronic

Between 1990 and 2005, the United States built 544 new prisons. That is an average of one new prison every 10 days.

databases and electronic fingerprint matching. In addition, police used financial tools, DNA matching, and security cameras. All of these things made it easier to convict people of crimes. Previously, those crimes may have been impossible to solve. However, critics point out that the rate of solved crimes has steadily decreased since the 1980s. For this reason, many experts believe other causes had a much larger effect on the prison population.

In the early 1970s, President Richard Nixon declared the War on Drugs. He convinced Congress to pass tough new drug laws. John Ehrlichman served as one of Nixon's advisers at the time. Ehrlichman later admitted that the drug laws were never meant to reduce drug use. Instead, they were meant to disrupt the people who opposed Nixon. Ehrlichman said Nixon

△ In 1971, President Richard Nixon claimed drug use was the biggest threat to the country.

felt threatened by anti-war **activists** and Black civil rights activists. Nixon knew marijuana was popular with anti-war activists. And he believed heroin was popular with Black leaders. So, Nixon hoped to imprison many of these activists for using drugs.

President Ronald Reagan continued the War on Drugs in the 1980s. He signed new laws that created even harsher punishments. In the 1990s, President Bill Clinton continued this trend.

To enforce drug laws, the US government started giving extra money to local police departments. Departments with higher arrest rates received more money. So, officers had a strong incentive to make lots of arrests. This policy led to a massive increase in the prison population. In 1970, only 400,000 people were arrested for drug crimes. By 2000, the number had reached 1.5 million.

Many experts also believe racism played a huge role in the growth of the prison system. A study from 1995 found that Black people made up 49 percent of those arrested for selling drugs. However, only 16 percent of drug dealers were

▲ Black people and white people use drugs at similar rates, but Black people are more likely to be arrested for it.

Black. That meant police were targeting Black people far more than white people. For this reason, Black people went to prison at much higher rates. The rise in the prison population was, to a large extent, a rise in the incarceration of Black men.

THE EFFECTS OF INCARCERATION

Life in prison is not easy. Being removed from society often harms prisoners' mental health. They may feel that their lives no longer have meaning. Also, many prisons are overcrowded. This can lead to various problems. For instance, diseases can spread more easily. Prisoners are also more likely to become violent.

Incarceration affects families, too. When a parent is behind bars, children are more likely to struggle with mental health. That can lead to problems in school. It can also lead to criminal activity. In addition, a person who is in prison cannot work. So, their family has less money. They may struggle to pay for food or housing.

The effects of incarceration continue long after people have finished their sentences.

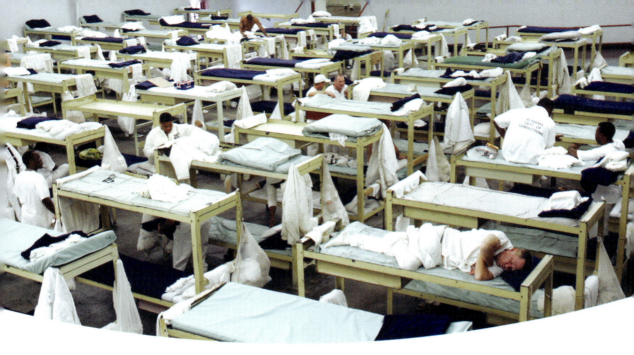

▲ Dozens of people are crowded into a large room at a prison in Alabama.

People convicted of **felonies** face several forms of legal discrimination. In many states, they cannot vote. Also, they cannot receive certain benefits. These include housing assistance, food assistance, and money for education. In addition, finding a job can be extremely difficult. That's because companies are allowed to ask people if they have a criminal record. For these reasons, many people experience homelessness after they get out of prison.

CHAPTER 5

GRADUAL DECLINE

By 2008, more than 2.3 million Americans were behind bars. That was the largest prison population in US history. But beginning in 2010, the number of prisoners began to decline. That had not happened in 40 years. Through the early 2020s, the prison population continued to fall gradually. Experts pointed to several reasons for this change.

In the 2010s, President Barack Obama worked to reduce mass incarceration.

▲ At the current rate of decline, experts believe it will take until 2093 to cut the US prison population in half.

One reason was the economy. The US economy struggled from 2008 to 2009. Many people and businesses earned less money during this period. As a result, the government did not collect as much money from taxes. This decrease forced the government to spend less on prisons. More than

100 prisons closed. Some prisoners were sent to other prisons. Other prisoners were released early.

Lower crime rates also played a role in the decrease. Rates of violent crime had been falling since the mid-1990s. For this reason, many people no longer saw crime as a major issue. So, Congress passed fewer laws to build new prisons.

People's attitudes about the War on Drugs began to change, too. In 1969, only 12 percent of Americans thought marijuana should be legal. By 2022, that number had risen to 68 percent. As of 2023, marijuana was legal in more than 20 states. Several other states had legalized it for medical use. As a result, fewer people went to prison for drug crimes.

Another reason was the shift toward alternatives to prison. For example, some states imprisoned fewer people convicted of nonviolent drug crimes. Rather than punishing people, these states focused on treating addiction. This method is far less expensive than incarceration. It also offers people more treatment options compared with what is available in prisons.

In addition, the American public became more aware of the role racism has played in the growth of the prison system. For instance, scholar David Garland coined the term "mass imprisonment" in 2001. And in 2010, author Michelle Alexander released *The New Jim Crow*. This book brought the term "mass incarceration" into common use.

Congress also passed the Fair Sentencing Act of 2010. Before this law took effect, people could be imprisoned for having very small amounts of crack cocaine. In contrast, people weren't imprisoned for having powder cocaine unless they had large amounts. On average, Black people were more likely to use crack cocaine. White people were more likely to use powder cocaine. For this reason, huge numbers of Black people went to prison. Meanwhile, many white people avoided prison. The Fair Sentencing Act helped reduce this disparity.

INCARCERATION RATES ◄

Despite a steady decline, Black people are still incarcerated at much higher rates than people of other racial and ethnic groups.

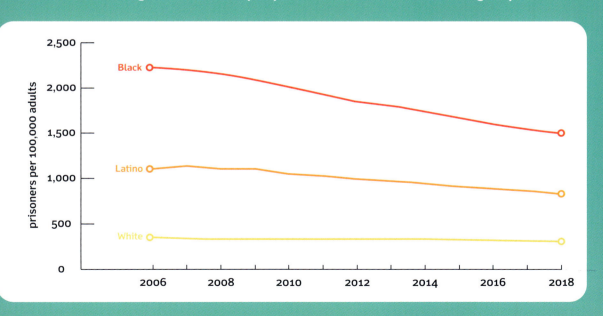

PRISONS FOR PROFIT

The government owns and operates most prisons. However, for-profit prisons are different. These prisons are businesses. Their goal is to make money. The government pays them to hold prisoners. A 2020 study found that 8 percent of US prisoners were in this type of facility.

For-profit prison companies often **lobby** Congress. They ask Congress to pass laws that will increase the rate of imprisonment. That way, they will make more money. For-profit prisons also make contracts with state and local governments. The contracts guarantee a minimum number of prisoners each year. As a result, police tend to arrest more people so they can satisfy the contracts.

In 2008, a for-profit prison became involved in the "kids for cash" scandal. Two Pennsylvania judges accepted $2.8 million in bribes from a

prison company. In exchange, the judges gave long, harsh sentences to hundreds of children. That way, the prison company would get more business.

Many critics believed similar scandals had happened in the past without being uncovered. They also believed similar scandals were likely to happen in the future. For these reasons, some activists hoped to ban for-profit prisons. However, as of 2023, the industry was still earning billions of dollars per year.

CHAPTER 6

JUVENILE INCARCERATION

Before the 1900s, **juvenile** prisoners were usually locked up with adults. The first juvenile court was created in the Chicago area in 1899. From that point on, many courts began treating children and teenagers differently from adults.

Today, most prisoners under the age of 18 are sent to juvenile prisons rather than adult prisons. Even so, approximately 10 percent of

A boy wears leg irons during a juvenile court case in Ohio.

juvenile prisoners are still locked up with adults. And in some cases, youth can be tried as adults and given adult sentences. Until 2005, some juveniles were even sentenced to death. However, a Supreme Court ruling ended this practice.

Every year, hundreds of thousands of young people end up in the criminal justice system. In most cases, their trouble begins in schools. Experts call this process the school-to-prison pipeline. It began in the late 1900s. At that time, many schools started using zero-tolerance policies. Under these policies, even small violations of the rules could result in heavy punishments. Zero-tolerance policies became most common in schools where a majority of students were people of color.

Many schools also hired school resource officers (SROs). These officers usually carry guns.

▲ More than 40 percent of public schools in the United States use SROs.

They also have the power to arrest students. For example, a student in Michigan was not wearing his school ID badge. An SRO took him to the principal's office. The school had a zero-tolerance policy. So, the student was suspended for one week. Then, as the student walked to the bus stop, another SRO arrested him for being outside of school. This type of result is not uncommon. Most of the arrests that SROs make are for minor violations. In contrast, minor violations rarely lead to arrest in schools without SROs.

Arrests often lead to serious consequences. Students who are arrested at school become part of the juvenile justice system. Courts can then order these students to follow strict rules. For instance, the students must not miss class. They must not disobey their teachers. If they do, they can be arrested again. When that happens, they are far more likely to end up in prison.

> ## THINK ABOUT IT

Do you think schools should have SROs? Why or why not?

▲ Students in New York City protest the school-to-prison pipeline in 2022.

The school-to-prison pipeline does not affect all students equally. Black youth are far more likely to be arrested than white youth, even when they break the same rules. Black youth make up more than 40 percent of the juvenile prison population. However, they make up only 15 percent of US youth overall.

CHAPTER 7

PUSHING FOR CHANGES

Activists argue that mass incarceration does not reduce crime. If it did, the United States would be one of the safest countries in the world. That's because the United States has one of the world's highest incarceration rates. But in reality, crime rates in the United States are similar to rates in other developed countries. And those countries have much lower rates of incarceration.

As of 2023, the United States had more than 6,000 prisons and jails.

To end mass incarceration, some activists are focusing on prison reform. These activists believe incarceration is still necessary in some cases. However, they want the number of prisoners to be greatly reduced.

One strategy is to stop crime before it starts. Researchers have found that crime is strongly linked to poverty. For this reason, many activists want to decrease funding for prisons. Instead, they want to use that money on things that can reduce poverty. Examples include education, affordable housing, health care, and job training. Social services such as childcare and food assistance can also help. Researchers have confirmed that these changes lead to lower crime rates.

Another strategy is to end mandatory minimum sentences. These are sentences that require

people to serve a certain amount of time in prison. States including Michigan and South Carolina ended mandatory minimums in the 2010s. This change led to a large decrease in the number of prisoners in those states. Over the same period, the states saw a decrease in crime.

Other activists say prison reform doesn't go far enough. They believe all prisons should be gradually shut down. These activists note that keeping people in prison does not undo the harm they caused. Also, researchers have found that incarceration does not decrease crime rates. Incarceration might also make some people more likely to commit crimes after they are released.

Instead, these activists want sentences to be based on **rehabilitation**. For instance, some people would receive addiction treatment. Others would receive mental health care. Others would receive education. Some people would receive all of these services.

> ## ➤ THINK ABOUT IT

Do you support stricter sentencing, prison reform, or closing prisons? Why?

Approximately six in ten victims of violent crime want prisoners to have shorter sentences along with rehabilitation.

This change would require a large number of workers. Paying them would be very expensive. However, activists point out that prisons are also very expensive. They say closing prisons would be a better use of taxpayers' money. They also believe it would offer more humane results.

FOCUS ON
MASS INCARCERATION

Write your answers on a separate piece of paper.

1. Write a letter to a friend explaining the main ideas of Chapter 4.

2. Do you think people should be put in prison for nonviolent drug crimes? Why or why not?

3. What do most experts believe is a major reason for mass incarceration?

    A. education
    B. racism
    C. mental health problems

4. Why are people more likely to experience homelessness after they get out of prison?

    A. They are arrested by school resource officers.
    B. They receive addiction treatment and mental health care.
    C. They face discrimination in housing, education, and jobs.

Answer key on page 48.

GLOSSARY

activists
People who take action to make social or political changes.

convicted
Found guilty of a crime.

disparities
Differences that are unfair.

federal
Having to do with the top level of government, involving the whole nation rather than just one state.

felonies
Crimes that the government considers serious, often punishable by time in prison.

incarceration
The act of keeping people in prison.

juvenile
Having to do with people under the age of 18.

lobby
To try to affect the decisions of lawmakers.

reformers
People who try to improve or fix problems.

rehabilitation
The process of returning to normal life, behavior, or activity.

solitary confinement
When a prisoner is kept apart from other prisoners.

TO LEARN MORE

BOOKS

Harris, Duchess, with Kate Conley. *The US Prison System and Prison Life*. Minneapolis: Abdo Publishing, 2020.

Harris, Duchess, with Cynthia Kennedy Henzel. *For-Profit Prisons*. Minneapolis: Abdo Publishing, 2020.

Lewis, Cicely. *Mass Incarceration, Black Men, and the Fight for Justice*. Minneapolis: Lerner Publishing, 2022.

NOTE TO EDUCATORS

Visit **www.focusreaders.com** to find lesson plans, activities, links, and other resources related to this title.

INDEX

Answer Key: 1. Answers will vary; **2.** Answers will vary; **3.** B; **4.** C